Money in the Community

Published in the United States of America by Cherry Lake Publishing
Ann Arbor, Michigan
www.cherrylakepublishing.com

Content Adviser: Danielle Peart, CPA
Reading Adviser: Cecilia Minden, PhD, Literacy expert and children's author
Book Design: Jennifer Wahi
Illustrator: Jeff Bane

Photo Credits: © mangpor2004/Shutterstock.com, 5; © Monkey Business Images/Shutterstock.com, 7; © Ivan Smuk/Shutterstock.com, 9; © Rawpixel.com/Shutterstock.com, 11; © Africa Studio/Shutterstock.com, 13; © Dragon Images/Shutterstock.com, 15; © violetkaipa/Shutterstock.com, 17; © Tyler Olson/Shutterstock.com, 19; © weerasak saeku/Shutterstock.com, 21; © legenda/Shutterstock.com, 23; Cover, 1, 6, 16, Jeff Bane

Library of Congress Cataloging-in-Publication Data

Names: Colby, Jennifer, 1971- author.
Title: Money in the community / Jennifer Colby.
Description: Ann Arbor : Cherry Lake Publishing, [2018] | Series: My guide to
    money | Includes bibliographical references and index.
Identifiers: LCCN 2018003328| ISBN 9781534129016 (hardcover) | ISBN
    9781534130715 (pdf) | ISBN 9781534132214 (pbk.) | ISBN 9781534133914
    (hosted ebook)
Subjects: LCSH: Finance, Public--Juvenile literature. | Taxation--Juvenile
    literature.
Classification: LCC HJ191.9 .C65 2018 | DDC 336.2--dc23
LC record available at https://lccn.loc.gov/2018003328

Printed in the United States of America
Corporate Graphics

About the author: Jennifer Colby is a school librarian in Michigan. She pays taxes and is also a public service worker.

About the illustrator: Jeff Bane and his two business partners own a studio along the American River in Folsom, California, home of the 1849 Gold Rush. When Jeff's not sketching or illustrating for clients, he's either swimming or kayaking in the river to relax.

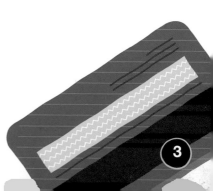

Do you go to a **public** school? Have you visited a public library? **Taxes** helped build these places.

What are other public places?

Taxes help public places. Public places can be parks. They can be roads and bridges.

Taxes help keep a public place clean. They help keep it safe. They help build more public places.

Everyone pays taxes. You pay taxes when you buy something. You pay taxes when you work.

Some people pay more taxes.
Some people pay less.

Form **1040** **U.S. Individual Income Tax Return** (99) **20**15

For the year Jan. 1–Dec. 31, 2015, or other tax year beginning _____ , 2015, ending _____ , 20 ___

Your first name and initial

Last name

If a joint return, spouse's first name and initial

Last name

Home address (number and street). If you have a P.O. box, see instructions.

Apt.

City, town or post office, state, and ZIP code. If you have a foreign address, also complete spaces below (see instructions).

Foreign country name

Foreign province/state/county

Foreign postal code

Tax and Credits

Standard Deduction for—
• People who check any box on line 39a or 39b who can be claimed as a dependent, see instructions.
• All other:
Single or Married filing separately, $6,300
Married filing jointly or Qualifying widow(er), $12,600
Head of household, $9,250

Filing Status

Check only one box.

1 ☐ Single
2 ☐ Married filing jointly (even if only one had income)
3 ☐ Married filing separately. Enter spouse's SSN above and full name here. ▶
4 ☐ Head of household (with qualifying person). (See instructions.) If the qualifying person is a child but not your dependent, enter this child's name here. ▶
5 ☐ Qualifying widow(er) with dependent child

Exemptions

6a ☐ **Yourself.** If someone can claim you as a dependent, **do not** check box 6a
b ☐ **Spouse**
c Dependents
(1) First name
(3) Dependent's relationship to you
(4) ✓ if child under age 17 qualifying for child tax credit (see instructions)

If more than four dependents, see instructions and check here ▶ ☐

d Total num...

Boxes checked on 6a and 6b
No. of children on 6c who:
• lived with you
• did not live with you due to divorce or separation (see instructions)
Dependents on 6c not entered above
Add numbers on lines above ▶

Income

Attach Form(s) W-2 here. Also attach Forms W-2G and 1099-R if tax was withheld.

If you did not get a W-2, see instructions.

7 Wages, sal...
8a Taxable in...
b Tax-exem...
9a Ordinary ...
b Qualified di...
10 Taxable refun...
11 Alimony receive...
12 Business income ...
13 Capital gain or (loss)...
14 Other gains or (losses)...
15a IRA distributions ...
16a Pensions and annuities ...
Rental real estate, royalties, par...
Farm income or (loss). Attach Sche... Schedule E
...yment compensation
...urity benefits 20a
...come. List type and amount
...the amounts in the far right column for li...
...expenses
...usiness expenses of reservists, performing artist...
...s government officials. Attach Form 2106 or 2106-E...
...th savings account deduction. Attach Form 8889
...oving expenses. Attach Form 3903
Deductible part of self-employment tax. Attach Schedule SE
Self-employed SEP, SIMPLE, and qualified plans
Self-employed health insurance deduction
Penalty on early withdrawal of savings
31a Alimony paid b Recipient's SSN ▶
32 IRA deduction
33 Student loan interest deduction
34 Tuition and fees. Attach Form 8917
35 Domestic production activities deduction. Attach Form 8903
36 Add lines 23 through 35 . . This is your **adjusted gross income**
37 Subtract line 36 from line 22.

7
8a
9a
10
11
12
13
14
15b
16b
17
18
19
20b
21
22
28
29
30
31a
32
33
34
35

People pay more taxes when they make more money.

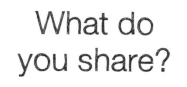

What do you share?

Your state charges people taxes. Sometimes your city does too. The **federal** government also charges taxes. This money is shared.

Taxes help pay public workers. These people are public school teachers. They are police. They are firefighters.

Taxes help **communities** grow. They help make **neighborhoods** better. Taxes help others.

Think of your city. Are there schools? Are there parks? What about a public pool? Ask an adult what their taxes pay for.

glossary

communities (kuh-MYOO-nih-teez) places and the people who live there

federal (FED-ur-uhl) relating to the government

neighborhoods (NAY-bur-hudz) small areas in a city where people live

public (PUHB-lik) open to or shared by all

taxes (TAKS-iz) money that a government requires people to pay

index

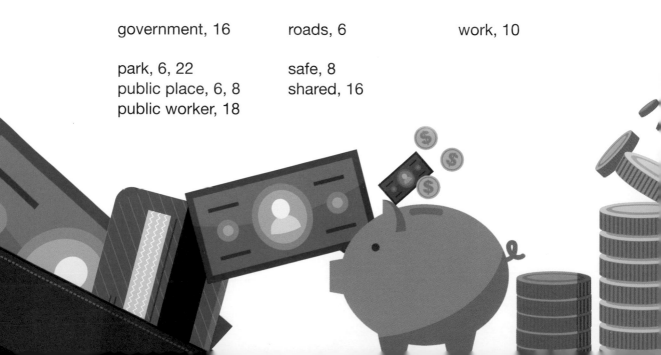